Dinosaur Publications

D1826985

# Migrating Birds

## by Peter Gill
illustrated by the author

Published by Dinosaur Publications Ltd, Over, Cambridge, Great Britain

© Dinosaur Publications 1982
© text and illustrations Peter Gill 1982

ISBN 0/85122/337-0  (paperback)
ISBN 0/85122/338-9  (hardback)
Made in Great Britain

When winter comes
swallows are no longer to be seen.
In olden days, people thought
the birds had curled up in the mud
at the bottom of ponds to sleep
until spring came again.

When Barnacle Geese came here in the winter,
people used to think that they had hatched
out of the goose barnacles which are
washed up on our beaches by the sea.
This is why they are called Barnacle Geese.

Now we know that
both these kinds of birds migrate.

Goose Barnacles

4

Many kinds of birds fly from one part of the world to another every year. This is called migration.

In springtime Swallows, Cuckoos, Warblers and many others arrive here to nest.

Chiff-chaff

Swallow

Cuckoo

The days are growing longer and warmer and there are lots of insects and other kinds of food in this country.

At the end of the summer, when the weather here gets colder again they fly away to another place where they can find plenty of food.

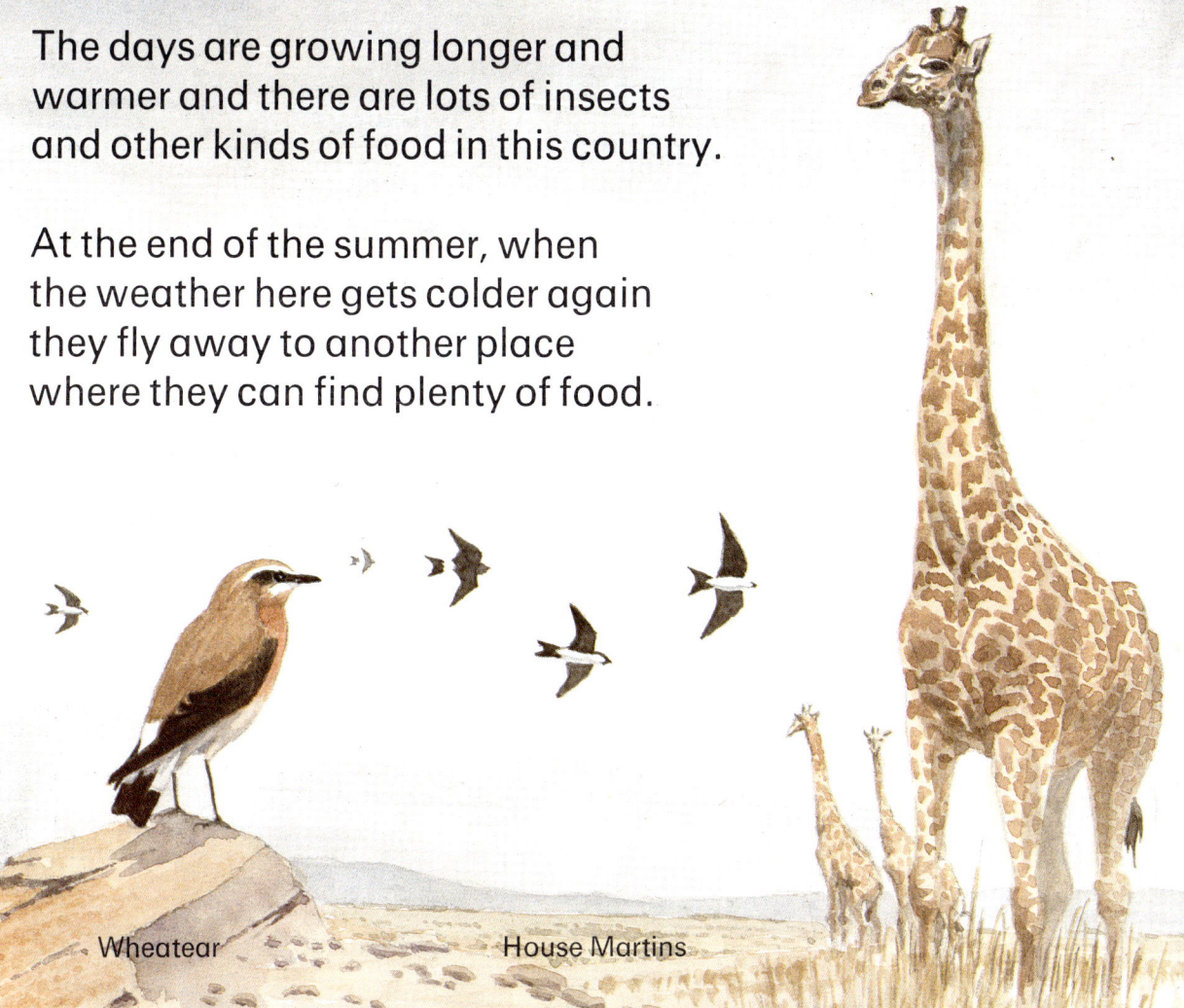

Wheatear                    House Martins

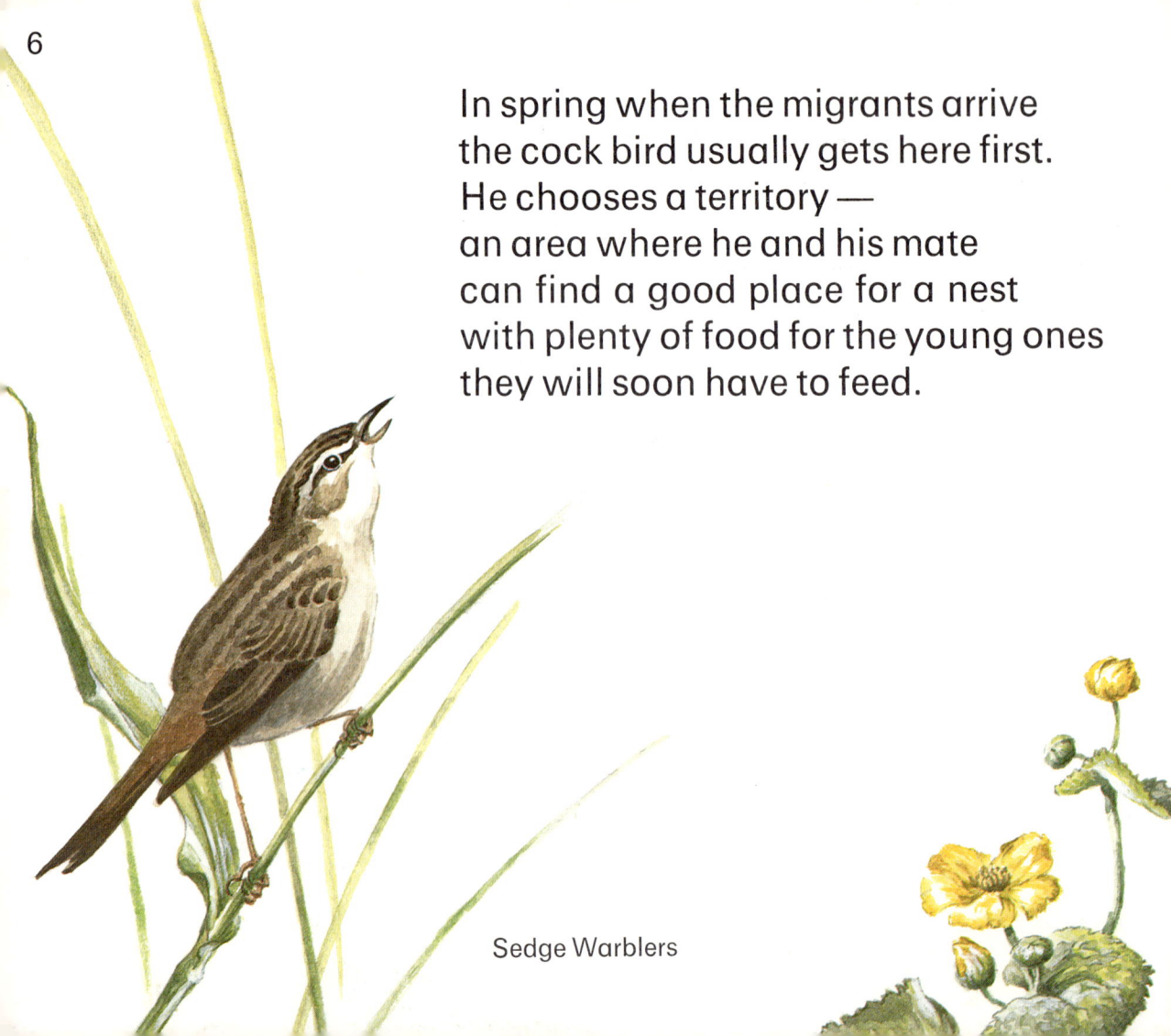

In spring when the migrants arrive
the cock bird usually gets here first.
He chooses a territory —
an area where he and his mate
can find a good place for a nest
with plenty of food for the young ones
they will soon have to feed.

Sedge Warblers

The cock bird keeps others away from
his territory by singing loudly and even
attacking them. When the hen birds
arrive they hear the singing
and soon choose a cock bird.
They start building a nest
and rearing a family together.

To get here many of these small birds
have flown thousands of miles
over jungle, desert and ocean.
Scientists who study birds think that
they find their way as sailors and
airmen do — by watching the sun and
the stars. If clouds hide the sun
or stars birds sometimes get confused
or lost.

Swallows

SOUTH
Midday

The sun rises in the East,
crosses the sky and sets
in the West. It is in the same
direction from us at
the same time each day,
so, with a good clock,
it is possible to steer
by the sun. Birds have
a very accurate 'clock'
in their brains.

Swallows

As birds get near their last year's home they seem to recognise familiar things like rivers, lakes and woodlands. The Swallow even finds its way to its own nest ! The Bewick's Swans which set off from northern Russia as winter draws near, find their way to the river or lake they know, bringing their cygnets with them.

Bewick's Swans

The long journey is full of dangers.
Some of the birds which set out
are blown in the wrong direction
and fall into the sea.
Some are caught and eaten
by birds of prey.

In countries where the laws do not
protect birds, many are shot and
trapped.

Eleanora's Falcon

Bird decoys

The young birds hatched here
in the spring soon grow up
and learn to find food
for themselves.

The parent birds moult,
losing their old, worn feathers
and growing new ones
so that they can fly
strongly.

Willow
Warblers

They all feed greedily,
growing a thick layer of fat
to give them the energy
they need for the journey ahead.

Some small birds are so fat when
they begin their migration that they
weigh twice as much as usual.

Layer
of fat

Sedge Warbler

As the days get shorter, groups of birds grow restless and begin to gather in flocks. Then, one day, when the wind can help them on their way, they set off on their long journey.

For many years, scientists have been catching and ringing birds. They clip a tiny metal ring with letters and numbers round the bird's leg. When a bird is caught again, by checking the records, they know where it came from.

Robin

Flocks of migrating birds can be
tracked by radar. In clear weather,
they can be seen by watchers
at the coastlines where the birds
start to cross the sea.

In these ways, we know that
most of our insect-eating birds
fly south to spend the winter in Africa,
beyond the Sahara desert,
five and a half thousand miles
away from Britain.

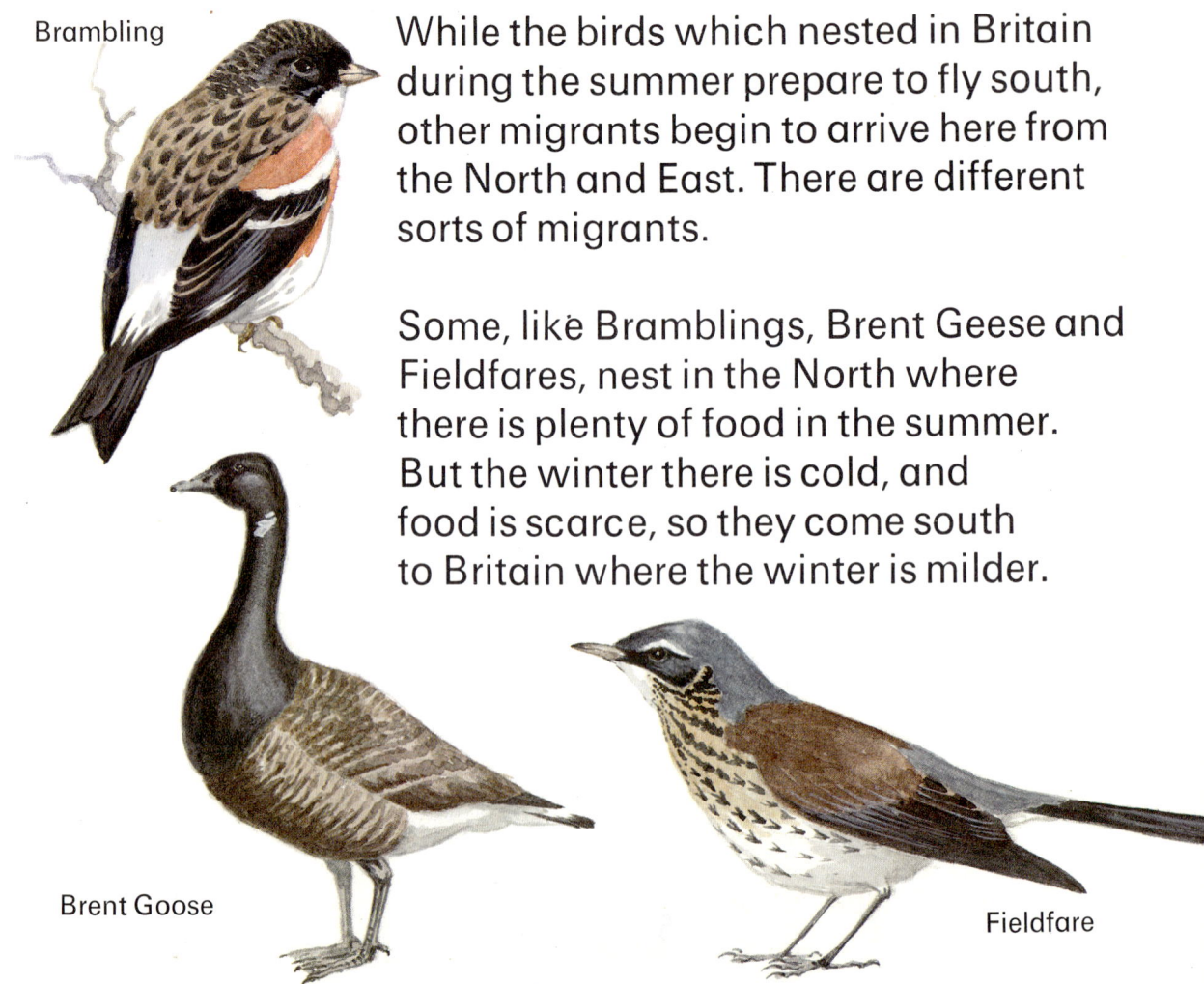

Brambling

While the birds which nested in Britain
during the summer prepare to fly south,
other migrants begin to arrive here from
the North and East. There are different
sorts of migrants.

Some, like Bramblings, Brent Geese and
Fieldfares, nest in the North where
there is plenty of food in the summer.
But the winter there is cold, and
food is scarce, so they come south
to Britain where the winter is milder.

Brent Goose

Fieldfare

Others, like the Wood Sandpiper and
Whimbrel, also nest in the far North.
They stop here to feed and rest
on their way to more southern
parts of the world.

Wood Sandpiper

Whimbrel

Starlings

Some other birds which nest
in the North, and come here
to escape from the cruel northern
winter, are of the same species
as birds we see all year.
Among these are vast flocks
of Starlings, and many Lapwings.

Lapwings

Even such familiar birds
as Robins and Chaffinches
migrate short distances.
Some arrive here from the North.
Some, which nested here,
move further south
to France and Spain.

Robin

Chaffinches

Kittiwake

Fulmar

Some seabirds which nest around
our shores also migrate in winter.
Kittiwakes and Fulmars wander
the North Atlantic and live at sea
through all the winter storms.
Petrels only come to land to breed
and spend most of their time
over the far South Atlantic.

Storm Petrels

The longest journey of all
is made by the Arctic Terns.
They nest as far north
as the Arctic Circle,
but during our winter,
some fly south to the edge
of the Antarctic ice.

Arctic Tern

In years when their food is scarce,
Waxwings and Crossbills come
from the continent in winter.

The Waxwings seek their
favourite rowan berries, while
the Crossbills feed on fir cone
seeds which they pick out
with their strange  crossed beaks.

Waxwings

Crossbills

In spring, migration starts again.
Our nesting visitors arrive
from the South to bring up
another family. Birds which spent
the winter here, now fly north
where the snow and ice
are melting.
Others can be seen again
as they rest here on their
long journey north.

Pied Flycatcher

Grey Plover

Snow Bunting

Caribou

Birds are not the only creatures
that migrate. Some animals do, like
the great herds of Caribou in North
America which move south each autumn.

Salmon hatch in streams and rivers.
They swim far out to sea to feed
and grow, then return to the same
streams to breed.

Even some insects migrate.
The Painted Lady butterfly migrates
from North Africa to Britain.

Painted Lady

Salmon

# "You insufferable, arrogant, infuriating man."

Just to make sure he didn't miss the point, Katlin went on. "I will tell you once more, Innishffarin will never be yours. Never. I am here to stay, and nothing—not absent servants or escaped horses and most especially not you—is going to make me leave. Is that clear?"

"Impeccably," Angus said. "In that case, madam, with your leave, I will be on my way." Almost as an afterthought, he said, "Incidentally, I think I know what it was that disturbed you in the passage."

"What?"

Angus smiled as he turned to go. Over his shoulder he said, "The ghost."

Katlin watched him disappear around the corner of the castle. She ran after him. He was almost at the stables by the time she caught up. Reaching out a hand, she grabbed hold of his arm.

"What ghost?" she demanded.

**Maura Seger** began writing stories as a child and hasn't stopped since. Her love for history is evident in the many historical romances she has produced throughout her career. A full-time writer, Maura experienced her very own romance in her courtship and marriage to her husband, Michael, with whom she lives in Connecticut, USA, along with their two children.